THE WAY, THE TRUTH & THE LIFE

Finding Joy, Peace, Power and Purpose in Jesus Christ

~~~~~~~ ✝ ~~~~~~~

Your Guide to Salvation

Copyright © 2020 Sandra Julian Barker
All Rights Reserved

Any unauthorized reprint or use of this material is prohibited without express written permission from the author and/or publisher.

Scripture quotations are from the New King James Version Bible, unless otherwise noted. Scripture taken from the New King James Version® - Copyright © 1970, 1980, 1982 by Thomas Nelson. Used by permission. All rights reserved.

Scripture quotations marked NIV are taken from the Holy Bible, New International Version, copyright © 1973, 1978, 1984 by International Bible Society. Used by permission of Zondervan Bible Publishing House. All rights reserved.

Scripture quotations marked KJV are taken from the Holy Bible, King James Version, translated in 1611, with copyrights, 1909, 1917, 1937, 1945 by Oxford University Press, Inc. All rights reserved.

Scripture quotations marked ESV are from The ESV® Bible (The Holy Bible, English Standard Version®), copyright© 2001 by Crossway, a publishing ministry of Good News Publishers. Used by permission. All rights reserved.

Photos by Sandra Julian Barker

Published by Joyful Writer Press
www.joyfulwriterpress.com
Chesapeake, Virginia
ISBN - 9798650133728

TABLE OF CONTENTS

Introduction	4
One: The Gift of Eternal Life in a Nutshell	8
Two: What's Stopping You?	10
Three: Unsure?	15
Four: Born Again? What's That About?	19
Five: Relationship and Religion	22
Six: How it All Began – Sin	26
Seven: God's Answer to Sin – Salvation	29
Eight: The Joy of Jesus – Truth to Set you Free	34
Nine: Know that you Know	39
Ten: Conclusion	41
Acknowledgements, Author Note & End Notes	44

"For God so loved the world
that He gave His only begotten Son,
that whoever believes in Him should not
perish but have everlasting life,"
John 3:16

✝

"Jesus said to him, 'I am the way,
the truth, and the life. No one comes to
the Father except through Me,'"
John 14:6

INTRODUCTION

The man asked, *"What must I do to be saved?"*
Acts 16:30

Here are two questions for you:
 -- Did you know that you can find joy, peace, power and purpose in your life if you do one thing?
 -- Would you be surprised to know that the kindest, most generous and loving person you've ever known is on the same path to hell as that unrepentant murderer – unless they do one thing?
 -- That one thing is to accept Jesus Christ as Savior.

Confess your sins and accept Christ's free gift of salvation and your final destination immediately changes from hell to heaven. Not only that, but you are immediately on a path that offers the joy, peace, power and purpose that you've been searching for all of your life.

This book will help you understand how simple and life-changing it is to accept Christ as Savior. You'll find answers to many questions you may have about what might seem like a mysterious thing to you. Please, read through this book with an open mind and heart and let God draw you to Himself. He loves you more than anyone on this earth could ever love you – always!

The Holy Bible makes it clear that *"All have sinned and come short of the glory of God"* and that *"All our righteousness is as filthy rags."* That makes "all" worthy of death and hell. The word "all" is totally inclusive of every man and woman who has ever taken a breath. Those aren't my words – they're God's words.

So, what hope do any of us have?

We have great hope! Because *"God so loved the world..."* we ALL have hope and that's Good News! You see, God offers each and every person the gift of life and forgiveness through the death of His Son.

The "one thing" we must do is to accept that gift, nothing more and nothing less. Continue reading this book and find out the answers you may have been asking; the answers that will help you become a Child of God, saved and born again – the one thing that is more important than anything else in the entire world.

In Scripture, God tells us, *"'You will seek Me and find Me, when you search for Me with all your heart, I will be found by you,' says the Lord,"* Jeremiah 29:13.

The way to Jesus is simple and free and God offers it to everyone. The Good News is that He offers this gift of eternal life to the worst offender, to the atheist, to the kind and gentle person -- to every person. He's eager for you to accept His free gift of salvation and a glorious life that never ends.

If you have never made that most important decision to ask Jesus Christ into your heart as your Savior, please, seriously consider His invitation to you. I guarantee you will *never* regret giving your heart to Jesus.

When you become a Child of the King, you will never regret your decision. A whole new wonderful world opens up for you and abundant life will begin - including those most sought after gifts of joy, peace, power and purpose.

Please, don't wait another day to say "Yes" to God's entreaty. The simple steps you need to take are in the next chapter.

In the book of Psalm, David writes: *"Preserve me, O God, for in You I put my trust...You will show me the path of life; in Your presence is fullness of joy; at Your right hand are pleasures forevermore"* 16:1 & 11.

God is love, God is hope, God is grace, God is peace and joy!

Jesus lovingly says, *"Come to Me, all you who labor and are heavy laden, and I will give you rest,"*
Matthew 11:28

Jesus said, "I have come that they may
have life, and that they may have
it more abundantly"
John 10:10

∞

"For I know the plans I have for you,
declares the Lord. Plans to prosper you
and not to harm you, plans to give
you hope and a future"
Jeremiah 29:11 NIV

CHAPTER ONE

THE GIFT OF ETERNAL LIFE IN A NUTSHELL

"For God so loved the world that He gave His only begotten Son, that whosoever believes in Him should not perish but have everlasting life," John 3:16

1 -Admit you are a sinner, unable to save yourself.

--"For all have sinned and fall short of the glory of God," Romans 3:23 NIV.
--"As it is written: There is no one righteous, not even one," Romans 2:10.
--"For the wages of sin is death..." Romans 6:23.

2 -As a sinner, you are condemned to die and go to hell someday. However, God loves you so much that He made a way for you to be freed from your sin, and to live and go to heaven to be with Him someday.

--"For God so loved the world that he gave His one and only Son, that whoever believes in Him shall not perish but have eternal life," John 3:16.
--"But God demonstrated His own love for us in this; while we were still sinners, Christ died for us," Romans 5:8.

3 --You cannot do anything to save yourself – no great work, nor life filled with good deeds. None of that can save you. Jesus is the only way.

--"For it is by grace you have been saved, through faith – and this not from yourselves, it is the gift of God, not by works, so that no one can boast" Ephesians 2:8-9.

--"He saved us, not because of righteous things we had done, but because of His mercy. He saved us through the washing of rebirth and renewal by the Holy Spirit" Titus 3:5.

--"Jesus said to him, 'I am the way, the truth, and the life. No one comes to the Father except through Me'" John 14:6.

4 --Salvation is a gift from a loving God, given through His perfect Son Jesus Christ, who paid the price for our sins by His death on the cross.

--"For the wages of sin is death, but the gift of God is eternal life in Christ Jesus our Lord" Romans 6:23

--"Yet to all who received Him, to those who believed in His name, He gave the right to become children of God" John 1:12.

5 -Believe that Jesus died for you and your sins, that He was buried and rose again the third day. Accept that gift, and you will be saved and become a child of God.

--"If you confess with your mouth, Jesus is Lord, and believe in your heart that God raised Him from the dead, you will be saved. For it is with your heart that you believe and are justified, and it is with your mouth that you confess and are saved" Romans 10:9-10.

--"Therefore, if anyone is in Christ, he is a new creation; the old has gone, the new has come!" 2 Corinthians 5:17.

It's that simple, yet many fail to accept that amazing, free gift, continuing instead to live a life without hope. Don't be one of them. Ask Jesus to save you this very minute! If you still have questions, keep reading.

CHAPTER TWO

WHAT'S STOPPING YOU?

How many people come to the crossroads of deciding for or against accepting Jesus as their Savior and say, "no?"

Way too many!

Jesus said, *"Enter by the narrow gate; for wide is the gate and broad is the way that leads to destruction, and there are many who go in by it. Because narrow is the gate and difficult is the way which leads to life, and there are few who find it"* Matthew 7:13-14.

Let's look at true stories of four people who came to that crossroad and let's examine their decisions. Two of these people lived and died nearly 2,000 years ago; one died a few years ago, and the other one is alive at the time this book was published.

A Jailer's Story

Nearly 2,000 years ago, the apostle Paul and his friend Silas were thrown into jail because they had cast a demon out of a girl in the power and name of Jesus.

At midnight, the two men were in their cell, praying and singing hymns of praise to God. The jailer and the other prisoners were all listening to the testimony of these men whose faith in God was evident by their words and behavior.

Suddenly, there was a great earthquake that shook open the doors of all the cells.

When the jailer realized all the prisoners had remained in their cells instead of escaping, he fell down trembling before Paul and Silas, and said, *"Sirs, what must I do to be saved?"* Acts 16:30.

Paul answered, *"Believe on the Lord Jesus Christ, and you will be saved."*

The jailer believed Paul's words. He took Paul to his house, where Paul preached the word of God to the jailer and those who were in his household, and they were all saved.

The story ends with these words about the jailer: *"and he rejoiced, having believed in God with all his household."*

King Agrippa's Story

Not long after Paul's experience in Philippi with the Jailer, he stood before King Agrippa (also called Herod) in the city of Caesarea. At the time, Paul was a prisoner of the Romans, because he had been falsely accused by the Jewish leaders.

Paul was happy to have the opportunity to present his case before King Agrippa, who was familiar with the customs of the Jews and seemed to have an open mind about the whole religious situation.

Paul told the king about his conversion from a Jesus-hater to a Jesus-follower and how he now preached repentance and the resurrection of Jesus.

Then Paul asked, *"King Agrippa, do you believe the prophets? I know that you do believe."*

The king answered, *"You almost persuade me to become a Christian,"* Acts 26:28.

Here is a man who heard the message of the gospel of Jesus and almost took the step of accepting Christ as his Savior. He was an intelligent ruler, yet he failed to take that most important step and sadly, he remained lost.

It is most likely that he is in hell today, because scripture tells us *"an angel of the Lord struck him, because he did not give glory to God. And he was eaten by worms and died,"* Acts 12:23. History records that the king died from intense stomach pains at the age of 54 years.

Anne's Story

Fast forward to the 21st century and let's look at the story of a young woman named Anne.

Anne was raised as a practicing Catholic who went to church each Sunday. She said, "I followed all the rules and never got involved in drugs, drinking or illicit sex. I wanted to make my family proud."

But her religion left her empty inside. She said, "I was desperately longing for something to make me happy. It seemed hopeless and so I resigned myself to a never-ending depressed state of life."

When she was a junior in college, Anne heard the personal testimony of two young men who shared their love for Christ through words and music.

She said, "My heart was touched and I longed for the happiness and fulfillment about which they spoke."

Later that night, Anne accepted Jesus as her Savior. She said, "I knelt beside my bed and talked to Jesus heart to heart. That night I was born-again. I actually felt God's love for the first time in my life and my attitude turned from one of depression to ecstatic joy. I really felt like a new human being and life was full of excitement."

Anne grew in her relationship with Jesus and enjoyed her Christian life on earth for over forty years. Just a few years ago, Anne died suddenly and without warning. Her last breath on earth was followed by her next breath in heaven where she is even now rejoicing with friends and family and her heavenly Father.

Anne died so suddenly that, if she had not already asked Jesus to save her, there would not have been time to do so. If she could send a message from heaven, there's no doubt she would warn anyone holding back on their decision to accept Christ – don't wait! Today is the day and now is the time! Be sure of your final destination!

Michelle's Story

Here's the story of a young woman who made a decision to accept Christ's offer of salvation and she continues to live with that wonderful knowledge every day of her life.

Michelle was unsaved and loaded down with baggage from her childhood and teen years. She married into a Christian family and observed a difference in their behavior and response to situations.

She began asking questions about the Bible and their belief system. Over a period of several years, asking questions and searching for peace, she realized she needed Jesus in her life.

One evening, after the funeral of a family member, Michelle approached her mother-in-law Susan and asked her how to be saved.

Susan happily told her the simple steps to salvation and asked Michelle if she wanted to ask Jesus to save her at that moment.

Michelle answered, "Yes, but I can't right now."

Susan asked, "What's stopping you?"

Michelle said, "I have to quit smoking first."

Susan smiled. "No, no you don't have to stop anything before being saved. Jesus came to seek and save those who are lost, no matter what their lives are like. You can be saved right now without doing a single other thing."

With those words of encouragement, Michelle breathed a sigh of relief and asked Jesus into her heart to save her. In that moment, she was gloriously born again into the family of God.

Her very countenance changed and she bubbled over with the freedom of Christ. She now knows a joy she'd never before experienced.

It's important to understand that you don't need to "clean up your act" before accepting God's free gift of salvation.

How About You?

There's a verse in Galatians that asks, "*Who hindered you from obeying the truth?* 5:7.

In each of these true stories, a decision had to be made. Three of the people accepted Jesus Christ as their Savior; one did not.

Don't become that one who did not.

"He who believes in the Son has everlasting life; and he who does not believe the Son shall not see life, but the wrath of God abides on him" John 3:36.

~Your Thots
--Which of these people do you most relate to?

--Is there something you think you have to give up before you can be saved?

--Below, compare Matthew 7:13-14 with a portion of poetry by Robert Frost. What similarities do you see?

 -Matthew 7:13-14: Jesus said, *"Enter by the narrow gate; for wide is the gate and broad is the way that leads to destruction, and there are many who go in by it. Because narrow is the gate and difficult is the way which leads to life, and there are few who find it."*

 -"I took the road less traveled, and it has made all the difference." Poem by Robert Frost.

--Which road are you on? Where is your final destination?

CHAPTER THREE

UNSURE

"Not everyone who says to Me, 'Lord, Lord,' shall enter the kingdom of heaven..." Matthew 7:21

Maybe you're still waffling on whether to ask Jesus to save you. Maybe, like King Agrippa, you say, "Almost you persuade me to be a Christian," but, maybe later.

Or, maybe, you once made a profession of faith, but you're not sure if you really meant what you said — perhaps you were just saying the words without a true change of heart. Are you an unsaved church-goer?

Or, you might be among the "worst offender" category of people — a thief, a murderer, or some other type of sinner and you wonder if God could ever forgive you.

Or, you might be wondering if the Bible is really true and accurate; is it really the Word of God?

Or, you might still be questioning the reality of this whole salvation thing. Is it real? Was Jesus really more than just a prophet and good guy? Is there really more to this world we're plowing through each day? Where's the proof?

Let's find answers to some of these important questions:

I'll Just Wait a While

Waiting puts you in mortal danger. As we saw in the story of Anne, death can come in the blink of an eye, and only those who are saved will go to heaven. Unless you settle your eternal destination before then, you may be lost forever.

Whether you believe in heaven and hell makes no difference to their reality. They are very real and your final destination *will* be one or the other.

The apostle Paul wrote, *"Behold, now is the accepted time; behold, now is the day of salvation"* 2 Corinthians 6:2. Now, today, this minute. Don't wait!

A Worst Offender and God's Grace

John Newton confessed to being one of those worst offenders. Born in London in 1725, John's life path was a rocky one, with painful twists and turns that were often caused by his headstrong disobedience and bad behavior.

As a sailor, John gained notoriety for being one of the most profane men his captain had ever met. Later, he became captain of a slave trading ship.

In spite of John's many sins, when he realized his lost condition and called out to God, "Lord, have mercy upon me!" the Lord heard his cry and saved him.

John became the beloved pastor of a church in England where he wrote the song, *Amazing Grace*, in 1773. That's quite a leap from his life as a cursing sailor and slave trader who scorned God. Amazing grace indeed!

Is the Bible Really Holy and True?

Some people simply don't believe the Bible is the true Word of God, while others think it's just a book of fairy tales. If you don't believe the Bible is true, how can you believe Christ died for your sins and you need to be saved?

The most famous evangelist of the 20th century was Billy Graham. You might be surprised to know that there was a time when he himself doubted the truth of the Bible. Here's a quote Billy gave in 1949:

"I had some young theologian friends who were expressing their doubts about the authority of the Bible. I began wondering if the Bible could be trusted completely.

"I began to study the subject intensively. Paul had written to Timothy, '*All scripture is given by inspiration from God.*' Jesus Himself had said, '*Heaven and earth shall pass away, but my Word shall not pass away.*' Jesus loved the scriptures and quoted from them constantly.

"I walked out in the moonlight, my heart heavy and burdened. I dropped to my knees and opened my Bible on a tree stump. If the issues were not settled soon, I knew I could not go on. 'O, God,' I prayed, 'There are many things in this book I do not understand. But, God, I am going to accept this book as your Word, by faith. I'm going to allow my faith to go beyond my intellect and believe that this is your inspired Word.'

"From that moment on, I have never doubted God's Word. When I quote the Bible, I believe I am quoting the very Word of God and there's an extra power in it."

Where's the Proof?

Salvation in Christ comes through faith. The definition of faith is found in Hebrews 11:1: "*Now faith is the substance of things hoped for, the evidence of things not seen.*" Further in that chapter, it says, "*But without faith it is impossible to please Him, for he who comes to God must believe that He is, and that He is a rewarder of those who diligently seek Him.*"

This is the basis of what Faith is – a belief with no proof. That's the way God created it to be and that's what He wants from us – Faith, without proof.

The famous author, C.S. Lewis, was once a determined atheist. After years of studying and seeking to know the truth, Lewis came to the conclusion that "faith is reasonable" and he became a believer.

Once he accepted Christ's sacrifice for him and was saved, his goal became to win others to this wonderful Christ.

Another atheist, Blaise Pascal, a French physicist, also struggled with Christian belief and God until he too was convinced of their reality and was saved.

Pascal wrote a famous piece called, *The Wager*. In it he wrote: "Belief is a wise wager. Granted that faith cannot be proved, what harm will come to you if you gamble on its truth and it proves false? If you gain, you gain all; if you lose, you lose nothing. Wager, then, without hesitation, that He exists."

For those who do not believe in heaven and hell, and the salvation of the soul through faith in Christ Jesus – what if you're wrong?

Whether you believe it's true, or not -- God *is* real. What you believe about Him does not make that fact any less true. But, what you believe about Him *will* determine your eternal destiny.

Faith is believing in something you cannot see. If you could see it and prove it, then it wouldn't be faith at all.

Faith may seem like a strange thing to unbelievers, but this is what God requires of His creation, whether you believe it or not.

God is so pleased when He sees faith in the hearts of His people, and He longs to reward such faith. Jesus said, "*I have come that they may have life, and that they may have it more abundantly,*" John 10:10.

Abundant life – isn't that what we all want? Abundant life is what God the Father offers to His children.

~Your Thots
-On a scale of 1 to 10 (with 10 meaning true faith), where do you land on the faith scale?

-What would it take for you to believe in Jesus as your Savior?

CHAPTER FOUR

BORN AGAIN?

WHAT'S THAT ABOUT?

Jesus said, *"You must be born again,"* John 3:7

How does one go about being "born again?" It sounds so mysterious!

In truth, it's not so mysterious and it's a beautiful process in becoming part of the family of God.

Let's look at the story of a man who was a religious leader during the time of the ministry of Jesus. Nicodemus was a Pharisee, well-educated in the scripture and all the laws of the Jewish religion, but he had questions.

Nicodemus had observed Jesus performing miracles and heard Him teaching. He was convinced Jesus had been sent by God, but there were things he didn't understand. This man was wise enough to go to the right place to find his answers. He was, however, just a bit hesitant for others to know of his interest, so he visited Jesus at night.

Nicodemus' Story

Nicodemus was following the Biblical command to *"seek and you shall find"* when he came to Jesus with his questions concerning salvation.

Jesus told him, *"Most assuredly, I say to you, unless one is born again, he cannot see the kingdom of God,"* John 3:3.

This was a concept that must have been new and strange to Nicodemus because he asked Jesus how a grown man could be born again since he surely couldn't enter his mother's womb again. The very thought of such a thing was preposterous!

Jesus patiently explained to him that the second birth was of a spiritual nature and not of a physical nature as was the first birth into the world as a baby.

Being born again involves an action of the heart. When a person accepts God's free gift of forgiveness by asking Jesus to save them from the punishment of their sin, the Holy Spirit works within that person's heart and changes it from "unsaved" to "saved." The person is immediately forgiven and *born again* into the family of God and becomes a child of God. *"Therefore, if anyone is in Christ, he is a new creation; the old has gone, the new has come!"* 2 Corinthians 5:17.

Instead of only being a child of whoever your earthly father and mother are, by being born again, you are spiritually born into the family of God and He becomes your heavenly Father. You have a spiritual as well as a physical family.

Whether you have (or had) a good father on earth, or not, your heavenly Father loves you totally and always wants what's best for you.

Not only does God become your Father, you are suddenly a part of a vast family of Christians who become your brothers and sisters. Each of you are joined in spirit by the bond of the Holy Spirit, who resides in every Christian.

When a person accepts Christ, there is a spiritual rebirth that is even more amazing and beautiful than the first physical birth as a baby, because this birth results in eternal life in heaven someday.

Growth After Rebirth

Just as a baby has much to learn and lots of growing to do before reaching adulthood, so also is there a need for spiritual growth when you are born again.

Paul speaks of new Christians being like a baby, still learning, still needing milk. As a Christian matures in knowledge and faith, they are able to understand more. In Hebrews 5, Paul says, *"For everyone who partakes only of milk is unskilled in the word of righteousness, for he is a babe. But solid food belongs to those who are of full age, that is, those who by reason of use have their senses exercised to discern both good and evil"* (verses 13-14).

How do you grow? There are several things that will help you grow and mature in your walk with God. Reading the Holy Bible which is God's very words in written form will help you learn the things about life, relationship and righteousness that He wants you to know and live by.

It's also important to talk with your Father often in prayer and to listen to Him speak to you in your spirit. It sounds mysterious, but it's God's way of communicating with His children and it has many benefits.

Listening to godly Bible teachers and preachers, spending time with other believers and helping others in God's name are all ways of growing in the Lord.

Growing in your spirit is an exciting and very satisfying journey which brings knowledge, peace and joy that the world can never give.

~Your Thots

--Does this explanation help you understand the second birth?

--Do you have more questions about it?

--Have you been born again?

CHAPTER FIVE

RELATIONSHIP AND RELIGION

> Religion gives us new laws; Christ gives us new hearts. Religion changes our appearances; Christ changes our natures. [from Heart to Heart, by Stephen Davey]

A person can be involved in Religion and have a personal Relationship with God as a born-again believer – and that's a good thing. But, the danger comes when a person is involved in Religion, but has never been born again and, therefore, does not and cannot have a personal relationship with God the Father.

Religion without Relationship is not only dangerous, it's downright deadly. Relationship is primary; religion is secondary.

So, what is the difference between the two?

Religion

The definition of Religion - is a social-cultural system of designated behaviors and practices, morals, worldviews, texts, sanctified places, that relate people to the supernatural.

That's a rather wordy way of saying that Religion is a system with rules and regulations, meant to help people be the best they can be before God. In truth, being the best we can be before God is never enough to make us righteous – *"We all fall short of the glory of God"* and *"All our righteousness is as filthy rags."* Religion is never enough.

Jesus Himself had some harsh words for the Religious leaders of His day. He was speaking to the very religious Pharisees and scribes when He said, *"Woe to you, scribes and Pharisees, hypocrites! For you cleanse the outside of the cup and dish, but inside they are full of extortion and self-indulgences...Woe to you, scribes and Pharisees, hypocrites! For you are like whitewashed tombs which indeed appear beautiful outwardly, but inside are full of dead men's bones and all uncleanness. Even so you also outwardly appear righteous to men, but inside you are full of hypocrisy and lawlessness"* Matthew 23:25 & 27-28.

Jesus was pointing out that actions speak louder than words. These hypocritical religious men knew scripture and sang praises to God, but their hearts were full of self-righteousness and judgmental attitudes. True worship was not even on their radar.

These verses offer a great illustration of a person who is Religious, with no Relationship to God.

Relationship

What is Relationship? Relationship is the way in which two people are connected; the way in which two or more people regard and behave toward each other.

Relationship is – acknowledgment – *"In all your ways acknowledge Him (God) and He shall direct your path."*

Relationship is to embrace a thing – that thing being salvation and a deepening connection with God. Jesus said, *"Abide in Me, and I in you. As the branch cannot bear fruit of itself, unless it abides in the vine, neither can you, unless you abide in me"* John 15:4. Now, that's relationship!

Jesus wants us to experience this amazing relationship so that we will have power and peace and joy. He said, *"These things I have spoken to you, that My joy may remain in you, and that your joy may be full"* John 15:11.

It's not just something on the outside (like religion can be) but it's inside the very deepest part of you.

We were created for Relationship with God. Adam and Eve had a beautiful relationship with God before sin came into the world and damaged that relationship. Some people search all their lives for something to fill that empty place in their lives, when the only thing that can fill it is the Holy Spirit of God – through accepting Jesus as Lord and Savior.

Why?

Why did Jesus leave heaven and come to the earth?

He answers that question in the book of Luke: *"For the Son of Man has come to seek and to save that which was lost,"* 19:10.

Those words of Jesus are simple, yet earth-shattering and life changing.

Lest you think it was easy for Jesus to become a man, consider that He was the everlasting King in heaven, adored and worshipped by angels, all powerful and almighty. He created all the stars in every universe, blew them into space and then named each and every one of them. This is power we cannot begin to comprehend.

Then, this almighty, beloved King deigned to step out from His glory and become a human on a dirt-filled, pain-filled, hate-filled earth. He allowed Himself to be bound by human physical frailty, to suffer, be beaten to a pulp and then painfully crucified by the very people He had created – all because of a love we cannot begin to comprehend.

Although His infinite love is beyond the understanding of our finite minds, we can accept it, rejoice in it and grow in it in beautiful ways.

All these things came to pass, because almighty God wanted a relationship with little ole you and me.

Religion vs Relationship

Those who are seeking God through Religion alone could be described, like Henry David Thoreau wrote, "The mass of men lead lives of quiet desperation."

People are desperate to find peace and relationship with God – and too often, they seek to find it through Religion alone.

It's possible to be a faithful member of a Church, and give it your all – and still have no relationship with God or peace in your heart.

Religion alone can leave you with no hope, no peace and no fulfillment, because, without a personal Relationship with Christ – Religion is empty. Neither baptism nor church membership can save you.

Relationship gives us hope, peace and fulfillment -- something Religion alone can never, ever provide.

So – is Religion a bad thing? Absolutely not! Religion coupled with personal Relationship with God is a powerful force God uses in this sinful world. Perspective is key. *"And whatever you do in word or deed, do all in the name of the Lord Jesus,"* Colossians 3:17.

The church is not just a building, it's the followers of God and He calls us "the bride of Christ."

When we have a personal Relationship with the Creator of the Universe, our Father God - we are Living Stones, Lights in the Darkness, Jars of Clay - filled with the Holy Spirit, the Salt of the earth, Strangers in this land – and Children of God. As John writes, *"Behold what manner of love the Father has bestowed on us, that we should be called children of God!"* 1 John 3:1.

~Your Thots

--In the old saying, "putting the cart before the horse," what represents the cart and what the horse when we think about religion and relationship?

--It is said that actions speak louder than words. Our actions are the outward expression of our inward affections. What does your outward behavior tell people about your inward beliefs and affections?

CHAPTER SIX

HOW IT ALL BEGAN - SIN

Life on Earth Begins

After God created the earth and everything on it, He set the first man and woman, Adam and Eve, in the beautiful garden called Eden. God told the young couple to enjoy everything in the garden except for one thing. They were forbidden to eat fruit from a tree called the tree of the knowledge of good and evil.

Here, we have a handsome man and beautiful woman living in a wonderful, perfect garden, with all manner of interesting and friendly animals. There are no mosquitoes to bite them, no thorns to prick their skin, no weeds to pluck. There is only beauty and enjoyment on every hand.

And, if that were not enough, Almighty God – their Father, came each evening and walked with them in the garden. Can you imagine conversing face to face with the great eternal God? Love and peace and joy would have surely radiated from Him. And, the things He must have discussed with them – talk about interesting!!

This was how it was meant to be. Because of that, every person is born with a yearning for a relationship with God. The Psalmist wrote: *"My soul thirsts for God, for the living God,"* 42:2. Most people don't know that's what keeps them searching for something they can't even name. There's a nagging sense of something missing; a feeling of – *there must be more to life than this*? The missing piece is that vital relationship with God. We're all born with an empty place inside our souls that can only be filled by God.

Fall of Man

In Genesis 3, everything changes and we read about the Fall of Man (the beginning of sin in the world).

Satan appears on the scene and does what he does best – he undermines God at every opportunity. He throws out that age-old question, *"Has God indeed said...?"*

Apparently, Lucifer aka Satan entered into a serpent and used him to speak to Eve. Here's how the conversation went between the serpent and the woman:

-**Satan's question**: *"Has God indeed said, 'You shall not eat of every tree of the garden'?"*

-**Eve's answer**: *"We may eat the fruit of the trees of the garden; but of the fruit of the tree which is in the midst of the garden, God has said, 'You shall not eat it, nor shall you touch it, lest you die.'"*

-**Satan's response**: *"You will not surely die. For God knows that in the day you eat of it your eyes will be opened, and you will be like God, knowing good and evil."*

Satan's words tempted Eve to want something more than she already had. Satan uses the same tactics today – and sadly, they still work.

The next verse changed the course of the entire world – not just for people, but animals and nature as well. *"So when the woman saw that the tree was good for food, that it was pleasant to the eyes and a tree desirable to make one wise, she took of its fruit and ate. She also gave to her husband with her, and he ate,"* 3:6.

Eve fell into sin and Adam tumbled down right behind her.

Dust to Dust

The rest of chapter 3 goes on to describe the shame Adam and Eve felt when God came to meet with them in the garden; and then the punishment God had to give them for their disobedience, and the dreadful curse that would hang over all mankind, as well as all of nature. It was the saddest day in history.

    Man would now toil and woman would know pain and sorrow; they would grow old and die and return to the dust. As if that weren't enough, they were then cast out of the beautiful garden home into a world that was suddenly filled with weeds and thistles. Sin affected all of creation. The animals who had once been their friends were now turned into wild creatures who would also die. Scripture tells us that all of nature "*groans*," as it awaits redemption from this curse.

    In spite of all this, God still loved these two people dearly – just as He loves you dearly. He made a promise to them that someday He would send One who would crush the serpent underfoot. This was the first reference to a Savior.

    From the first failure of woman and man to trust and obey, all of humanity has followed in their footsteps. I'm so thankful God didn't give up on us and that He eventually sent His Son to crush the head of the old serpent, shed His own innocent blood, and provide a way for us to regain our relationship with God that had been so badly damaged in those early days.

    Two thousand years ago, the promise God gave to Adam and Eve was fulfilled through the death and resurrection of Jesus Christ our Savior.

~Your Thots
--Compare the statement on page 9, with a statement made by St. Augustine.

   -from page 9: "We're all born with an empty place inside our souls that can only be filled by God."

   -St. Augustine: "You have made us for yourself, O God, and our hearts are restless until they find their rest in you."

--What does this mean to you?

CHAPTER SEVEN

GOD'S ANSWER TO SIN – SALVATION

In one sentence we see the cure for sin: Salvation through Jesus Christ is God's answer to sin.

Let me elaborate. The Bible's definition of "Salvation," is deliverance from sin and its consequences brought about by faith in the shed blood of Jesus Christ for the payment of that sin.

After Adam and Eve had disobeyed God and brought sin into the world, our merciful heavenly Father gave them a promise. He said to Satan: *"And I will put enmity between you and the woman, and between your seed and her Seed; He shall bruise your head, and you shall bruise His heel,"* Genesis 3:15.

From the very beginning, God revealed His plan to redeem His fallen creation from the curse of sin. His promised Redeemer would be born of a woman and someday He would crush Satan's head.

Over and over in the Old Testament of the Bible, God gave prophecies and promises about the perfect Redeemer that He would one day send to earth to be a Savior.

In the fullness of time, God sent His only perfect Son to be born on the earth and live as a man. When Jesus was 30 years old, He began His earthly ministry, telling people about His Father, about repentance from sin and about salvation.

After three years of ministry, Jesus, who was perfect and innocent of any wrong, was put to death on a cross in the

City of Jerusalem. While He was on the cross, He asked His Father in heaven to forgive those who had crucified Him.

At one point during the crucifixion, God the Father turned His back on His Son for the first and only time ever. At that moment, Christ, who was sinless, was bearing every sin of every person who ever lived – past, present and future – upon His perfect self. He was paying the price for all those sins with His life as payment. God cannot look upon sin and so He turned His back on His beloved Son until the price was paid by His death. Jesus became the perfect Lamb of God, shedding His blood and paying the price for sin, because the wages, or price of sin is death. Jesus paid that price so that you and I do not have to.

When God accepted that payment for sin, Jesus cried out, "It is finished!" He then gave up His Spirit and His body died.

Jesus' friends buried Him in a tomb and rolled a massive rock across the opening. Roman soldiers sealed the tomb and kept watch there because they feared His followers would steal His body away.

The soldiers were shocked when they witnessed the appearance of angels who rolled the stone away and announced that Jesus was no longer in the grave because He had risen from the dead.

      The soldiers were horrified and ran away. Only a few hours later, friends of Jesus came to the tomb and found that it was empty. Jesus had risen from the dead, just as He said He would do. After His resurrection, He walked on earth and met with His followers for 40 days before ascending up to heaven. He has promised to come again someday – someday very soon!

A Deeper Look at the Way of Salvation

~ All have Sinned~
  --"For all have sinned and fall short of the glory of God," Romans 3:23.
  --"As it is written: There is no one righteous, not even one," Romans 2:10.

~ Result of Sin ~
  --"For the wages of sin is death..." Romans 6:23.

~ Believe that God Loves You and Christ Died for You ~
  --"For God so loved the world that he gave His one and only Son, that whoever believes in Him shall not perish but have eternal life," John 3:16.
  --"But God demonstrated His own love for us in this; while we were still sinners, Christ died for us," Romans 5:8.

~ Good Works or Being Good Can Not Save ~
  --"For it is by grace you have been saved, through faith – and this not from yourselves, it is the gift of God, not by works, so that no one can boast," Ephesians 2:8-9.
  --"We are all like an unclean thing, and all our righteousness is like filthy rags," Isaiah 64:6.
  --"He saved us, not because of righteous things we had done, but because of His mercy. He saved us through the washing of rebirth and renewal by the Holy Spirit," Titus 3:5.

~ Salvation is a Gift We All Need ~

--"For the wages of sin is death, but the gift of God is eternal life in Christ Jesus our Lord," Romans 6:23

--"Yet to all who received Him, to those who believed in His name, He gave the right to become children of God," John 1:12.

--"Jesus answered and said to him, 'Most assuredly, I say to you, unless one is born again, he cannot see the kingdom of God,'" John 3:3.

~There is Only One Way~

--"Jesus said to him, 'I am the way, the truth, and the life. No one comes to the Father except through Me,'" John 14:6.

--Jesus said, "Enter by the narrow gate; for wide is the gate and broad is the way that leads to destruction, and there are many who go in by it. Because narrow is the gate and difficult is the way which leads to life, and there are few who find it," Matthew 7:13-14.

--"If you confess with your mouth, Jesus is Lord, and believe in your heart that God raised Him from the dead, you will be saved. For it is with your heart that you believe and are justified, and it is with your mouth that you confess and are saved," Romans 10:9-10

~ We Become New Creations When We are Born Again ~
 --"Therefore, if anyone is in Christ, he is a new creation; the old has gone, the new has come!" 2 Corinthians 5:17.
 --"We love Him because He first loved us," 1 John 4:19.
 --"Likewise, I say to you, there is joy in the presence of the angels of God over one sinner who repents," John 15:10.

~Once Saved Always Saved~
--Once a person has trusted in Jesus Christ as his or her Savior from sin, that person remains sealed by the Holy Spirit of God and will always be a part of the family of God – always! You cannot lose your salvation. Once saved – always saved.
--"In Him you also trusted, after you heard the word of truth, the gospel of your salvation; in whom also, having believed, you were sealed with the Holy Spirit of promise, who is the guarantee of our inheritance until the redemption..." Ephesians 1:13-14.

~Baptism~
--Baptism is not required to be saved. Baptism is an act of obedience and witness to the world that a person who is saved has died to their old self and been raised to new life in Christ. Although not required, it is a step of obedience.
--The thief on the cross beside Jesus asked Jesus to save him and Jesus answered, "Today you will be with me in paradise," Luke 23:43. The thief was never baptized, yet he was saved and went to heaven.

 Jesus says to us: "Come unto me, all you who labor and are heavy laden, and I will give you rest," Matthew 11:28

Scripture in this Plan of Salvation is taken from the NIV translation of the Holy Bible.

CHAPTER EIGHT

THE JOY OF JESUS – TRUTH TO SET YOU FREE

Jesus said, *"You shall know the truth and the truth shall make you free,"* John 8:32.

Scripture tells us that someday there will be the thunderous sound of every knee bowing before our Lord and Savior Jesus Christ. He is the true and eternal King of kings and He is worthy of all of our praise!

In the meantime, those of us who have accepted this kind and loving Jesus as our Savior are blessed to have Him as part of our lives on a daily basis.

There is more Joy in belonging to Jesus and walking with Him than anything the earth could ever offer.

Psalm 16:11 says, *"You will show me the path of life; in Your presence is fullness of joy; at your right hand are pleasures forevermore."*

In John 15, Jesus offers a parable about a grape vine and the vital importance of each branch remaining attached to the vine. He said, *"I am the true vine...Abide in Me, and I in you...for without Me you can do nothing...Abide in my love."*

He ended by saying, *"These things I have spoken to you, that My joy may remain in you, and that your joy may be full."*

The Good Shepherd

From the beginning, Jesus was slated to be the perfect Lamb of God who would take away the sins of the world.

All through the Old Testament, up until the day of Jesus' death, the blood of unblemished lambs was required for the forgiveness of sin.

Jesus became that spotless lamb. When John saw Him, he said, "*Behold! The Lamb of God who takes away the sin of the world!*"

We humans are so like sheep in many ways and so God often compares us to them. "*All we like sheep have gone astray; we have turned, every one, to his own way; and the Lord has laid on Him the iniquity of us all,*" Isaiah 53:6.

Just before Jesus was taken prisoner by the soldiers, He told his dear disciple Peter, "*I tell you, Peter, the rooster shall not crow this day before you will deny three times that you know me,*" Luke 22:34.

Jesus knew that His dear friend would betray Him that very night, yet He loved Peter and was praying for him that his faith would be strengthened.

In spite of our wandering, Jesus is our good shepherd. He forgives us and loves us through thick and thin and cares for our every need.

So, Who is this Wonderful Jesus?

Colossians 1:15-20ESV gives a description of some of the supernatural attributes of who Jesus is – here are a few of them:

--"*He is the image of the invisible God...*" This means that when we read the words of Jesus, when we see His actions that are described in scripture and when we sense His power and love, we are also seeing what God the Father is like. Although the Father and the Spirit are invisible, the Son bears their image in His being, which helps in our pursuit of a personal relationship with God.

-- "*...all things were created through Him and for Him. And He is before all things, and in Him all things hold together.*"

Wow! This is one of those amazing wonders that we don't totally understand, but we can totally rejoice in because we know that our Savior Jesus is Almighty in every way and in control of everything – and He loves us beyond imagination.

-- "*He is…the firstborn from the dead…*" Although Jesus and even the disciples raised people from the dead, each of those people eventually died again. Jesus was the first and only person who has risen from the dead and continues to live. His death and resurrection offer a picture of what will happen someday when the dead in Christ are raised from their graves by Jesus Himself. They too will live forever with the Lord.

The Truth

Jesus Himself said, "*I am the way, the truth and the life. No one comes to the Father except through me,*" John 14:6.

In a court of law, witnesses are required to promise to "tell the whole truth and nothing but the truth, so help you God." We all want the truth.

At one point in His ministry, Jesus prayed aloud for His followers, saying to God, "*Sanctify them by Your truth. Your word is truth,*" John 17:17.

When Jesus says He loves you with an everlasting love and promises you a home in heaven with Him, you can stake your life on the truth of His words. And you can rejoice in the truth of the children's song: "Jesus loves me this I know, for the Bible tells me so."

God IS love. "*Greater love has no one than this, than to lay down one's life for his friends,*" John 15:13. And that's what Jesus did for each of us.

~Your Thots

--Compare John 1:1-4 with Colossians 1:15-17. What similarities do you see?

--Read John 1:14. Who is the living Word?

--In what similar ways do the Word of God (the Bible) and the living Word (Jesus) point us to God?

CHAPTER NINE

KNOW THAT YOU KNOW

"We are more than conquerors through Him who loved us," Romans 8:37

The verse on the pictured cross is in Psalm 138:8-NIV

"Therefore, if anyone is in Christ, he is a new creation; old things have passed away; behold, all things have become new," 2 Corinthians 5:17.

Once you ask Jesus Christ into your heart to save you from sin, you are born anew into the family of God. The Holy Spirit, which is part of God, enters into your heart and offers you a comfort, peace and joy that you never knew before. He will never leave you or forsake you; He will always be there to offer guidance and He will empower you to do things you never thought possible.

He will be with you in life and in death.

It sounds mysterious, and in a way it is, but it's also totally real and totally wonderful!

If you have experienced this change in your heart, then you may know that you are saved and on your way to heaven someday. Rejoice in that knowledge!

If you have not experienced this change of heart, then it's time to examine yourself and check to see if you have asked Jesus to save you, or not. After all, it's the most important thing a person can ever do during their lifetime.

"These things I have written to you who believe in the name of the Son of God, that you may know that you have eternal life..." 1 John 5:13.

Knowing that you know brings a peace and joy that is beyond anything the earth can offer.

When David speaks of God in Psalm, he says, *"You will show me the path of life; in Your presence is fullness of joy; at Your right hand are pleasures forevermore,"* 16:11.

"Being confident of this very thing, that He who has begun a good work in you will complete it until the day of Jesus Christ," Philippians 1:6.

~Your Thots
--Read Romans 8:35-39 and answer the question, *"Who shall separate us from the love of Christ?"*

--Do you know that you know that Jesus is your Savior and you belong to Him?

CHAPTER TEN

CONCLUSION

"And take the helmet of salvation, and the sword of the Spirit, which is the word of God; praying always..."
Ephesians 6:17-18

Peter was speaking of Jesus Christ when he wrote, *"Whom having not seen you love. Though now you do not see Him, yet believing you rejoice with joy inexpressible and full of glory, receiving the end of your faith – the salvation of your souls,"* 1 Peter 1:8-9.

Ah! The *"salvation of your souls"* – that thing that is worth more than all the treasures the world could ever offer.

Remember, the Biblical definition of Salvation is deliverance from sin and its consequences, brought about by faith in the finished work of Jesus Christ.

Without Salvation, we have to pay the consequences for our own sins, which is death. With Salvation, our sin debt was paid by the shed blood of Jesus Christ and we have life and freedom.

This then is what it is all about -- Salvation. Without it, we'll never enter heaven. With it, we become a part of the family of God Himself and inherit eternal life in heaven.

How could there ever be a question about choosing Salvation?

Grow in Christ

Once you've accepted Christ as Savior, it's important to grow as a Christian. Reading the Holy Bible, God's Words to His people, is the best way to start.

"All Scripture is given by inspiration of God, and is profitable for doctrine, for reproof, for correction, for instruction in righteousness, that the man (or woman) of God may be complete, thoroughly equipped for every good work" 2 Timothy 3:16-17.

Reading good devotional books, listening to good preachers and Christian music, praying, and spending time with other Christians are all good ways to continue to grow in this wonderful new life that God has given you.

"That you may walk worthy of the Lord, fully pleasing Him, being fruitful in every good work and increasing in the knowledge of God, strengthened with all might, according to His glorious power..." Colossians 1:10-11.

Let me leave you with words Jesus spoke to His followers – words recorded by the apostle John – words to live by and cherish as we walk with our Lord:

"Abide in Me, and I in you. As the branch cannot bear fruit of itself, unless it abides in the vine, neither can you,

unless you abide in Me...for without Me you can do nothing...abide in My love," John 15:4-5.

"*Rejoice in the Lord always. Again I will say, rejoice!*" Philippians 4:4.

Suggestions for Growth as a Child of God

First and foremost, reading the Holy Bible since it is God's direct words to His people. I suggest you might begin with the books of Genesis, Psalm, the four Gospels of Matthew, Mark, Luke and John, Acts, Philippians and Galatians.

Good Bible studies are highly recommended, such as *Chase the Lion*, by Mark Batterson; *Ancient Treasure – Old Testament Gems*, by Sandra Julian Barker; *Heaven*, by Randy Alcorn; and *My Heart's Desire*, by David Jeremiah.

Find a good, gospel teaching church and go each Sunday. Listen to good preachers on the radio, YouTube, or podcasts. David Jeremiah, Robert Jeffress, and Stephen Davey are good examples.

✯✯✯ ✝ ✯✯✯

If you have made the decision to ask Jesus into your heart to save you, welcome to the family of God, dear brother or sister! I would love to hear from you so that I may rejoice with you and personally welcome you into our family of God. Or, if you have questions about anything in this booklet, just drop me an email at joyfulwriter@hotmail.com. I would love to send you additional material that will help you grow in the Lord.

May God bless you and make His face to shine
upon you and give you peace.

Acknowledgements
Author Note & End Notes

Acknowledgements

Thank you to those who helped with proof reading this manuscript and offering valuable input on how to make it better. Your help is so appreciated! Special thanks to Larry B, Ava, Sandy B., Steven, Norm, Sara. Larry G, and Peggy T.

All praise King Jesus!

Author

Sandra Julian Barker is a student of God's Word, enjoying Bible studies by well-known teachers such as Beth Moore, Priscilla Shirer, Mark Batterson, and many others. She is a Sunday school teacher, women's ministry leader in her church, and a speaker with the group *Women Victorious*. She is author of a number of books, including *Ordinary Women – Extraordinary God,* volumes one and two; *Joy in the Journey,* and *Ancient Treasure – Old Testament Gems*. Her books are available on Amazon. Her greatest desire is to encourage hurting hearts, and to point others to the saving knowledge of our wonderful Lord and Savior, Jesus Christ and to a victorious life. To God be the glory!

Her blog is: Sandra-ramblingrose.blogspot.com

End Notes

--Photos by Sandra Julian Barker unless otherwise noted.
--page 5: photo from stained glass window in Christ's Church, New Bern, NC.
--page 12: Robert Frost, American poet; poem excerpt from *The Road Not Taken*, published in The Atlantic Monthly in August 1915.
--page 14: C. S. Lewis (1898-1963), British writer and lay theologian, quote from *The Screwtape Letters*, published by Geoffrey Bles, 1942.

Blaise Pascal (1623-1662), French philosopher and mathematician, "The Wager" in *Pensees*, 1657-58.

--page 19: "Religion gives us new laws; Christ gives us new hearts. Religion changes our appearances; Christ changes our natures" from Heart to Heart, by Stephen Davey, Heart to Heart Magazine, published by Wisdom International, May 2020.

--page 22: Henry David Thoreau (1817-1862), essayist, poet, philosopher; quote written in 1845, published in *Walden's Pond*.

--page 25: Adam & Eve carving, artwork in church in Aarhus, Denmark.

--page 26: St. Augustine of Hippo (A.D. 354-430) was an Algerian-Roman philosopher and theologian of the late Roman / early Medieval period.

--page 28: photo of stained glass at St. Giles Cathedral, Edinburgh, Scotland.

--page 30: photo of stained glass at St. Giles Cathedral, Edinburgh, Scotland.

--page 32: photo of stained glass in St. Mary's Catholic Church, Fredericksburg, Texas.

--page 39: photo from stained glass window in R.E. Lee Memorial church (ca 1840), Lexington, VA.